Damaged

Damaged

H. Waldon

Alex Zandrea Books

To the survivors, warriors in their fight,
You are not alone.

CONTENTS

CONTENTS

CONTENTS

CONTENTS

Dear Reader,

These verses are not merely ink on paper; they are fragments of my soul, an attempt to breathe life into the shadows that once consumed me. I invite you into the recesses of my heart, where darkness and light engage in a relentless dance. Each line, each stanza, is a testament to the silent battles I fought in the hidden corridors of an abusive relationship. The pain etched into these words is the residue of the storms I weathered, the echoes of silent screams that reverberated within my being. I share these poems not to seek pity but to break the silence that often shrouds such experiences. It is a cathartic unraveling of emotions, an acknowledgment of the haunting journey that I, and many others, have traversed.

Through the verses, I yearn to convey the complexity of emotions — the fear that shackles, the longing for liberation, and the internal conflict that accompanies the decision to stay or leave. It is a raw exposure of vulnerability, a narrative that speaks not only of pain but also of resilience. May these poems be a whisper to those who have faced similar shadows, a reminder that they are not alone. And to those who haven't tread these darkened paths, may these words offer insight into the silent struggles that often go unnoticed.

In sharing this darkness, I aspire to kindle a spark of understanding and empathy. For it is through shared stories that we can illuminate the path toward healing and hope.

With gratitude,

H. Waldon

National Domestic Violence Hotline is available 24 hours a day, seven days a week.

800-799-7233

or text START to 88788

thehotline.org

Part One

The Dance of Illusions

In the realm of whispered promises, she dwells,
A woman wrapped in dreams, where longing swells.
Her heart, a captive to a love untold,
A tale of passion, fragile and bold.

In shadows cast by unrequited desire,
She weaves a tapestry, fueled by the fire.
For him, a beacon in her twilight sky,
A love that blooms, yet withers, passing by.

He was the melody in her silent song,
A phantom dance where she'd always belong.
But he, a wanderer in the night,
Elusive, like the fading morning light.

Her love, a painting on a shifting breeze,
A masterpiece painted with silent pleas.
Yet, he was a muse, free and untamed,
In her heart, an echo that softly named.

She held his laughter in the crystal air,
Yet he slipped through fingers, like strands of hair.
In the garden of her heart, he'd never sown,
Yet the seeds of love had wildly grown.

A dance of echoes, in the hush of night,

She loved a man who lingered out of sight.
Though never hers, she clung to the illusion,
A bittersweet dance, a love's confusion.

He, a ship that sailed on distant seas,
A silent whisper carried by the breeze.
Her love, a lighthouse on a distant shore,
Guiding him home, forevermore.

Through the mist of tears, she'd often trace,
The silhouette of love, a fleeting embrace.
For in her heart, a tale of love's refrain,
A woman loved a man, but loved in vain.

Paradox of Longing

In the mirror's gaze, I find a weary soul,
A wanderer haunted by a fear untold.
In the silent echoes of my heart's abyss,
Abandonment's shadow, a relentless twist.

A tapestry woven with threads of doubt,
In the labyrinth of fears, I find my route.
Each bond a fragile, delicate thread,
Trembling, fearing, on a path I tread.

From the cradle of love to life's vast sea,
Abandonment's ghost has followed me.
In the dance of relationships, a hesitant waltz,
I fear the sting of love's sudden faults.

A whispered promise, a silent vow,
Yet, within me, seeds of doubt would plow.
In the warmth of affection, I find a chill,
A fear that time will bend, and hearts will still.

Scars etched deep, like chapters in a book,
Every goodbye, a haunted, lingering look.
Yet, I crave the closeness, the tender touch,
Caught in a paradox, I love too much.

In the silence of night, where shadows weep,

Abandonment's specter, a secret I keep.
I build walls high, yet yearn to connect,
A paradox of longing, I try to dissect.

But let me find solace in a tender gaze,
A love unbroken, defying life's maze.
For in the arms of trust, I long to find,
A sanctuary for my heart, a peace of mind.

In the fragile dance of healing's embrace,
I'll rewrite the story, find a resting place.
Though abandonment whispers, a constant hum,
I'll paint my own sunrise, declare I've overcome.

Echoes of Agony

In the silence, where words become the knife,
I bear the weight of a turbulent life.
A love, once vibrant, now cloaked in pain,
In the echoes of abuse, I wear a chain.

Each syllable, a lash upon my soul,
A tempest of torment taking its toll.
Your words, like acid, etch upon my heart,
A masterpiece of agony, tearing me apart.

In the quiet spaces where tears reside,
I'm shackled to a love I cannot hide.
A prisoner of your venomous voice,
I'm lost in a storm, with no other choice.

Beneath your rage, my spirit starts to fray,
Yet, in your darkness, I choose to stay.
A captive to the echoes of cruel disdain,
In the wreckage of love, I remain.

Your anger, a tempest that never calms,
Leaving scars, like haunting psalms.
I dance on eggshells, afraid to speak,
In the ruins of love, my heart grows weak.

Each insult, a wound that never heals,

In the battlefield of love, where silence steals.
Yet, in the rubble of dreams, I search for light,
Hoping for dawn to break through the night.

For the heart that's battered, yet refuses to break,
Yearns for a love that's not built on heartache.
In the ruins of pain, where emotions run wild,
I'm still aching for the tenderness of a gentle smile.

So, I gather strength from the shards of my soul,
To break free from a love that takes its toll.
For in the wreckage of a verbal storm,
I'll find my voice, and let it transform.

In the tears that fall, and the courage I find,
I'll reclaim a love that's gentle and kind.
In the echo of healing, I'll redefine,
A love that's built on words that bind.

Absence

In the quiet of the night, my heart weeps,
A symphony of longing, as loneliness seeps.
I'm adrift in the echoes of what used to be,
Missing you, though you may not miss me.

Moonlight dances on the fragments of my dreams,
As I navigate the vastness, where silence teems.
I reach for memories, like petals in the breeze,
Yet, in this void, my heart finds no ease.

Your absence echoes in the chambers of my soul,
A haunting melody, an ache that takes its toll.
Do you feel the void, the space I once filled?
Or in your world, am I easily distilled?

I trace the constellations, seeking your gaze,
Wondering if, in your heart, I still have a place.
The stars above, witnesses to my silent plea,
Missing someone who probably doesn't miss me.

In the silence, I wrap myself in memories,
Chasing shadows of your laughter like gentle seas.
Yet, the truth emerges, stark and cold,
I'm a chapter in your story, left untold.

The distance between us, an ocean wide,

Yet, in my heart, you're by my side.
Do you sense the void, the empty space?
Or does time erase every lingering trace?

Missing you is a bitter, tender art,
A masterpiece painted with a breaking heart.
In the echo of silence, my tears find release,
Missing someone who probably doesn't miss me.

The Bruised

In shadows deep, where secrets hide,
She walked a path with tears as her guide.
A heart once free, now chained in despair,
In a love that whispered, yet stripped her bare.

He wore a mask of a charming guise,
Yet within his touch, a storm would rise.
A dance of pain, a relentless waltz,
As his anger struck, his love would false.

In the mirror's gaze, her reflection wept,
A soul shattered, promises unkept.
Bruises painted a tale of silent cries,
A canvas of agony, in her haunted eyes.

The echoes of his words, like shards of glass,
Piercing her spirit, shattering the mass.
Yet, she clung to hope in the darkest night,
Hoping for dawn, for a glimmer of light.

In the hushed corners, where silence dwelled,
Her heart whispered secrets, never to be quelled.
A prisoner of love, a captive of fear,
She longed for a haven, for someone near.

Each step she took, a cautious ballet,

In a labyrinth of pain, she lost her way.
Yet, in her eyes, a flicker remained,
A silent plea for love unrestrained.

In the wreckage of dreams, she sought release,
A phoenix longing for a soothing peace.
Her heart's lament, a tear-stained song,
In the symphony of abuse, she danced along.

But within the ruins, resilience grew,
A whisper of courage, a strength anew.
She gathered the fragments of her broken core,
To escape the torment, to breathe once more.

In the quiet escape, she found her voice,
A survivor's anthem, a powerful choice.
For in the embers of heartbreak's pyre,
She rediscovered herself, her soul on fire.

A Dreamer's Anthem

In the quiet corners of my restless mind,
A tempest of shadows, love's ties unbind.
Bound by chains of an abusive embrace,
I yearn for liberation, a different space.

He, the orchestrator of a brutal ballet,
Dances on the stage of a love in decay.
In his anger, I find no refuge or peace,
A captive soul seeking sweet release.

Longing for another, a distant dream,
In the realms of fantasy, a love redeemed.
He, a savior in the guise of another,
A beacon of hope in this love's cruel smother.

I close my eyes, escape to a world unseen,
Where love is gentle, where hearts convene.
In the arms of a dream, I find solace and grace,
A haven where love wears a kinder face.

He, my rescuer in the shadows' retreat,
Whispers of tenderness, a melody sweet.
In the dreamscape, he dries the tears I've shed,
A savior from a love that left me bled.

Yet, in the waking hours, reality bites,

The chains of abuse, the endless fights.
I long for escape, to break the binds,
But fear's icy fingers crawl up my spine.

The dream dissolves, replaced by cold truth,
A love that devours the flames of youth.
Yet, as I yearn for another's touch,
He senses the shift, the change as such.

His eyes, a storm of suspicion and ire,
He senses the pull of my heart's desire.
Accusations fly, like arrows aimed true,
He blames me, the scapegoat he construes.

In the cyclone of rage, a tempest untamed,
He hurls words, a symphony of pain.
"Whore," he spits, a venomous decree,
A label that chains, a verdict on me.

I tremble, a leaf in the storm's cruel gust,
As his anger erupts, a relentless thrust.
Blaming me for the cracks in our love's foundation,
He denies his role, his violent aberration.

In the labyrinth of guilt, I find myself lost,
A hostage to blame, at an unimaginable cost.
Yet, in the crevices of my fractured soul,
I yearn for a love that can make me whole.

As I navigate the shadows of my plight,
I gather strength, for the dawn of my flight.
For in the crucible of dreams and despair,
I must find a way out, breathe in fresh air.

Bound

In the shadows, I am tethered, a captive soul,
Entwined in a dance where darkness takes control.
Silent screams echo within my chest,
A symphony of agony, an unending quest.

He wears a mask, a deceptive guise,
Yet behind closed doors, love is the compromise.
Bruises hidden beneath a cloak of shame,
In this twisted waltz, I'm bound by his name.

A prisoner of whispers that cut like knives,
In the labyrinth of fear, my spirit strives.
To break free from chains that silently bind,
Yet the escape seems a dream, impossible to find.

In the hallowed silence where secrets reside,
I fear the daylight, where truths are implied.
For leaving holds echoes of an unknown strife,
A step into darkness, away from this life.

The world outside, a tempest unknown,
But within these walls, agony is my own.
A paradox of yearning for freedom's embrace,
Yet terrified that leaving is a perilous chase.

A fragile hope clings to each passing day,

Yet the shadows lengthen, and courage gives way.
For leaving is a maze, a labyrinth unknown,
With monsters lurking in the fields I've never sown.

What awaits beyond this suffocating night?
Will freedom heal or ignite a fiercer fight?
In the crevices of fear, I'm entangled and torn,
Afraid that leaving means facing a storm.

The world may judge, but they can't comprehend,
The complexities of a heart that's condemned.
In the quiet rebellion of my silent cries,
I'm trapped in a web where freedom denies.

Oh, how I long for a whisper of grace,
A chance to break free from this heart-wrenching place.
But in the shadows, I'm held by the chains,
A captive, entangled in love's bitter remains.

Masks and Missteps

In the hushed aftermath of the storm,
A tempest brewed, emotions forlorn.
I made a mistake, a tragic misstep,
Igniting a conflict, a regrettable bet.

Words, like knives, cut through the air,
A verbal dance, a cruel affair.
He said what stung, a venomous dart,
A reaction ignited, tearing apart.

In the echo of anger, a reflex untamed,
I slapped him, my actions unclaimed.
Yet, in an instant, the tables turned,
His fist met my flesh, the lesson learned.

A dance of chaos, a symphony of pain,
A narrative spun in a toxic refrain.
Guilt wrapped around, a suffocating shroud,
In the aftermath, silence was loud.

The morning light unveiled the toll,
A blackened canvas, the mark took hold.
The mirror reflected a brutal truth,
A testament to the clash of anger and youth.

I crafted a tale for curious eyes,

A web of lies, veiling the cries.
To coworkers, I painted a different scene,
A fragile facade, a misleading sheen.

"It's just a clumsy stumble," I would claim,
A misstep in darkness, a story to tame.
Yet, behind the makeup, the carefully drawn guise,
Lies the canvas of pain, where the truth belies.

In the hollow echoes of my silent plea,
I grapple with the weight of what could be.
For in this labyrinth of self-blame,
I'm lost in a cycle, a dangerous game.

A blackened eye conceals the shame,
A secret tale etched in bruised flame.
In the broken mirror, I face the truth,
A survivor's journey, seeking a healing soothe.

The First Confession

In the shadows of a love, fragile and worn,
A woman stands, a heart deeply torn.
The man she loves, a tempest in despair,
A revelation unveiled, a confession laid bare.

For years, the chains of abuse held tight,
Yet love lingered in the depths of the night.
His eyes, once a harbor, now stormy seas,
Revealed a truth, a battle to appease.

One fateful night, a confession spilled,
A relapse into darkness, a promise unfulfilled.
In the hallowed space of their shared despair,
He bared his soul, his demons laid bare.

"I've fallen again," his words echoed deep,
A secret unveiled, emotions to reap.
Her heart, a canvas painted with scars,
Yet love persisted, like distant stars.

"Get help," she implored, a plea in her eyes,
To break the chains, to sever the ties.
He, defiant, claimed strength of his own,
To face the demons, to stand alone.

In the echoes of confession, a truth unfolds,

A love story written in shadows and molds.
She, with a heart battered, questioned why,
Love lingered even as tears blurred the sky.

Intensity gripped her, emotions ran wild,
In the storm of love, a helpless child.
The paradox of love, a confusing flame,
Even as it burnt, she clung to its name.

Through the wreckage of dreams, hope persisted,
A love story twisted, emotionally twisted.
For in the broken fragments, love's ember glowed,
A question unanswered, a mystery untold.

In the labyrinth of pain, she stood strong,
A melody of love, a bittersweet song.
As he vowed to change, to break free,
She pondered the why of her love's decree.

Love, a paradox, with no clear rhyme,
Yet she held on, through the ebb and climb.
For in the heart's chaos, a truth unfurled,
She loved him, despite the tumultuous world.

Silent Screams

In the battlefield of words, we dance,
He and I, trapped in this toxic trance.
For years, I've swallowed the bitter taste,
Of his anger, his venom, a relentless waste.

A silent vow to avoid the fray,
I tiptoe through words, careful what I say.
Yet he, a storm that rages unbridled,
Verbal blades unsheathed, emotions compiled.

Nonstop, the torrent of cruel disdain,
A cascade of torment, a relentless rain.
Walking on eggshells, a precarious art,
Yet his words persist, tearing me apart.

In the labyrinth of silence, I navigate,
A minefield of triggers, a venomous debate.
But patience wears thin, a fragile thread,
As he hurls one more insult, I see red.

A hairbrush becomes my silent plea,
A projectile aimed to set me free.
Yet his response, a hurricane of rage,
A torrent of violence, a brutal stage.

Against the wall, hands around my throat,

A dance of darkness, a life's boat afloat.
In the other room, my son, just six,
Unseen witness to this heart-wrenching fix.

His eyes reflect the terror I feel,
Yet, in my silence, the pain I conceal.
In the suffocating grasp of a love diseased,
I yearn for freedom, for a moment's ease.

As the storm subsides, and he releases his grip,
I am left bruised, broken, in silence I slip.
For my son's sake, I wear a mask,
Concealing the torment, the shadows unasked.

In the quiet hours, I ponder the cost,
Of a love that's shattered, irreparably lost.
For in the echoes of the night's cruel tide,
I dream of escape, of a place to hide.

Blame Took Root

Once, in the echoes of laughter, we twirled,
A love so vibrant, a canvas unfurled.
Yet now, shadows linger, in silence they creep,
As I unravel the tapestry, memories we keep.

In the beginning, a symphony of bliss,
A dance of hearts, sealed with a kiss.
His eyes sparkled, a promise untold,
But now, in their depths, a tempest unfolds.

A tale of happiness, once etched in our gaze,
Now eclipsed by storms, in tumultuous haze.
He was a prince, in love's warm embrace,
But now, a monster, consumed by rage.

Jealousy, a poison, seeped through his veins,
Igniting fury, breaking love's reins.
Every word, every glance, a spark to ignite,
The inferno of anger, a relentless fight.

I try to remember when the darkness took hold,
When happiness shattered, and love grew cold.
A lie, a deceit, a fracture unseen,
The roots of the poison, where love careened.

Caught in a web of my own fabrication,

I ignited the storm, the catalyst of desolation.
He, a victim of my deceitful dance,
His love turned wrath, a painful trance.

In the quiet moments, I question my fate,
As I navigate a love, a twisted debate.
Where did we lose the laughter, the joy?
When did our love become a broken toy?

His eyes, once mirrors of adoration,
Now reflect a turbulent desperation.
I mourn the man he used to be,
Lost in the labyrinth of our shared history.

Yet, the blame lies heavy on my soul,
For I sowed the seeds that took their toll.
In the ruins of love, I search for a clue,
To the moment when joy bid adieu.

As the storms rage on, I hold onto hope,
In the echoes of love, I try to cope.
For in the wreckage of what used to be,
I yearn for a glimpse of the man he was to me.

Unseen Chains

In the shadows of despair, I stand,
Bound by chains, in love's cruel command.
A whispered hope echoes in the night,
Yet self-doubt clings, an oppressive blight.

The mirror reflects a shattered soul,
A narrative of pain, a heart's heavy toll.
I yearn to escape, to break the chains,
Yet the voice within, relentless, remains.

In the dance of darkness, I feel confined,
A captive heart, a love maligned.
The echoes of abuse, a haunting refrain,
Yet the belief lingers, I'm not worth the gain.

The bruises hidden, beneath the skin,
Tell a story of battles, of love's cruel din.
In the caverns of my heart, self-worth crumbles,
A silent plea in the night softly mumbles.

"I'm not enough," the whispers persist,
A narrative etched, a love dismissed.
In the labyrinth of doubt, I navigate,
A prisoner of fear, in love's cruel state.

The world outside, a daunting space,

I fear rejection, love's cold embrace.
No solace in the arms of another,
For who would want a soul to smother?

I convince myself, this is my fate,
To endure the torment, accept the weight.
The belief entrenched, an insidious seed,
That in love's garden, I'm but a weed.

In the hollows of my heart, a silent cry,
A plea for freedom, a desperate sigh.
Yet the chains tighten, the voice persists,
"You're not enough," a cruel twist.

But in the shadows, a flicker of light,
A yearning for a different fight.
For within me, a strength concealed,
A truth untold, a love revealed.

I am enough, deserving of more,
To break free from the shadows that implore.
In the echoes of doubt, a resilience stirs,
A silent rebellion, a soul that prefers.

To cast away the shackles that bind,
And in the vast unknown, my worth to find.
For in the depths of despair, a truth takes hold,
I am enough, a story yet untold.

Triggered Storm

In the dim-lit room where shadows creep,
A couple tangled in a dance, love's secrets to keep.
Fingers point, words sting like a whip,
A storm of anger, a volatile trip.

She speaks a truth he cannot bear,
The room transforms into a battleground, a despair.
A shove, a punch, the air grows dense,
Violence erupts, a dreadful sequence.

Her body crashes onto the unforgiving bed,
The echo of pain in the words unsaid.
A punch lands hard on her fragile jaw,
Silent screams in the violence withdraw.

He, a tempest of rage, unchecked,
Choking the life from a love long wrecked.
In the room, a roommate, an unwitting witness,
To the symphony of violence, a crescendo of distress.

She cries out, a plea in the silent night,
For salvation from this brutal fight.
Yet, the walls stand witness, cold and mute,
As violence claims love, an unholy pursuit.

In the echoes of brutality, a cry is born,

A testament to a love, twisted and torn.
The room, a chamber of horrors untold,
Where the heart, once warm, turns cold.

In the aftermath, bruises tell the tale,
A canvas of pain, love's tragic derail.
As she lies broken, the room bears witness,
To the aftermath of a love in distress.

A chilling silence lingers in the air,
Love, now a relic beyond repair.
The room, a witness to a tragedy untold,
Where violence weaves a narrative, dark and cold.

Despair

In the garden of shared laughter, a proposal unveiled,
A glimmer of hope in love's intricate tale.
He, on bended knee, a ring in hand,
A promise whispered, love's steadfast stand.

She, eyes glistening with tears unshed,
A breath caught in the dance of hearts unfed.
The proposal, a moment frozen in time,
Yet beneath the surface, shadows would climb.

Emotion surged as she realized the truth,
Love's tender blossom, tainted by the uncouth.
A veneer of normalcy, a fleeting illusion,
In the depths of love, a turbulent confusion.

The ring, a symbol of vows unspoken,
Yet shadows linger, promises broken.
As they left the friend's embrace,
A storm brewed, love's familiar trace.

Fingers pointed, words hurled like knives,
In the aftershocks of love, passion thrives.
A fight ensued, a tempest unbound,
In the battleground of love, emotions drowned.

She, caught in the maelstrom of despair,

Heart heavy with burdens, love threadbare.
The proposal's glow, a distant ember,
As love, once promising, began to dismember.

The fight raged on, a relentless strife,
A recurring theme in the symphony of their life.
She, weary of the battles, the endless debate,
Tears mingling with the rain, a love's cruel fate.

In the turmoil, she yanked off the ring,
A metallic clatter, a symbolic fling.
Into the yard, the symbol cast,
A love story unraveling, fading fast.

The air hung heavy with love's lament,
As the ring lay in the grass, love's testament.
They, never destined to break free,
In the echoes of the fight, love's tragedy.

She, with a heart heavy and burdened,
In the rain-soaked yard, love's fate overturned.
The proposal's memory tainted by despair,
As she walked away from a love threadbare.

Masquerade

In the masquerade of joy, a facade I wear,
A smile painted, love's illusion to declare.
To the world, I showcase a perfect embrace,
Yet behind closed doors, a darker space.

In the eyes of friends, a love story divine,
A tale of happiness, a narrative so fine.
Yet beneath the surface, shadows entwine,
A silent scream, a love maligned.

He, the great man, in the public eye,
Yet behind the curtain, a different guy.
A tempest of violence, a toxic storm,
In the silent corners, my heart takes form.

I wear a mask, a smile so bright,
To shield the truth, to hide the fight.
To my family's ears, a tale spun,
Of love's triumphs, not battles won.

The bruises concealed, beneath the guise,
In the labyrinth of secrets, my heart complies.
I dance in the shadows, my pain unseen,
A master of disguise, love's tragic sheen.

In the tapestry of deceit, emotions weaved,

A tale of happiness, yet love deceived.
To the world, a picture so complete,
Yet in my heart, a silent defeat.

A prisoner of silence, I play my part,
A puppeteer's dance, a soul torn apart.
In the symphony of lies, a solo played,
A love story tainted, emotionally frayed.

In the daylight's glare, the act persists,
A painted smile, a love's amethyst.
Yet in the night, when shadows loom,
I face the truth, the silent room.

In the echoes of pain, emotions collide,
A love concealed, a spirit denied.
Yet I yearn for a dawn, a new refrain,
To break free from the chains of love's cruel game.

For in the masquerade, a truth unfolds,
A heart in silence, a story untold.
In the depths of secrecy, I find my plea,
To unmask the pain, to set love free.

Captive Soul

In the echoes of laughter, we left the party's cheer,
A storm brewing in silence, whispers in the rear.
He, a tempest unbound, resentment in his gaze,
A fuse ignited, love's delicate phase.

In the car's confines, tension brewed,
Unspoken words, emotions subdued.
On the highway of turmoil, we traveled home,
In the shadows of anger, love was overthrown.

A fire sparked, a fuse ready to ignite,
His anger, a tempest, a hurricane's bite.
As his voice crescendoed, an ominous tune,
I was entangled in the chords of our love's monsoon.

He pulled the car to a sudden halt,
A battleground chosen, emotions in assault.
I stepped out, into the night's cold embrace,
Unaware of the storm, the fury he'd chase.

In the dim-lit road, the drama unfurled,
As he chased me down, in the underworld.
His fingers, like shackles, gripped my hair,
A captive soul in the tangle of despair.

Dragged back to the car, like a puppet on strings,

In the shadows, echoes of silent screams.
The door slammed shut, my hair caught in the strife,
A prisoner of love, a twisted dance for life.

Emotions swirled, a tempest within,
A tumult of fear, love's unraveling hymn.
In the cramped back seat, a prisoner I lay,
Hair entwined in the door's cold dismay.

Tears welled up, pain etched on my face,
A captive of love, in this darkened space.
Physically trapped, emotionally torn,
In the wreckage of love, a soul worn.

The car moved forward, the night closing in,
A journey through darkness, a path unforeseen.
I yearned for escape, a break from the fight,
To untangle the strands of our love's bitter plight.

Tired of the battles, the endless war,
I wished for an end, for pain no more.
In the silence that followed, an internal plea,
For liberation from chains, to finally be free.

As the car drove on, shadows embraced,
A captive soul yearning for a different space.
In the echoes of love, a silent plea,
For freedom to reign, for love to be free.

Broken Glass

A weight-lifting echo in the dim-lit space,
A shattering of glass, a break in grace.
She steps into the shards, pain on display,
A query tossed to him in the light's dimming ray.

"Do you know of this broken glass?" she inquired,
A mystery unraveling, the truth desired.
He denied, a poker-faced charade,
In the garage's shadows, secrets laid.

The glass, a metaphor for truths concealed,
A dance of deception, a fate revealed.
Symbolic shards, scattered and sharp,
A connection to secrets, a truth to harp.

A puzzle unfolded, pieces unaligned,
In the wreckage of trust, a mystery entwined.
He denies, she questions, a ritual to repeat,
The broken glass whispers, secrets to unseat.

A silent witness to a tale untold,
The garage's secret, a story to unfold.
Shattered trust like the glass on the floor,
A mystery persists, love's fragile core.

Symbolism etched in each shard's gleam,

Connected to secrets, a broken dream.
In the garage's dimness, truth obscured,
A puzzle unsolved, a soul disturbed.

The broken glass, a silent plea,
For honesty, for trust, for love to be free.
Yet in the shadows, secrets reside,
In the mystery of broken glass, love hides.

Veiled Absence

Amidst a sea of silver and navy hues,
A love story unfolded, vows to choose.
Years of trials, a journey long,
He conquered demons, emerged strong.

The bride adorned in a strapless grace,
A vision of beauty, a delicate embrace.
The scent of flowers, a fragrant tide,
Petals whispered secrets, love as their guide.

A silvered veil, cascading and fine,
Adorned the bride, in love's design.
With every step, the aisle she graced,
Years of love, in the moment embraced.

The ceremony, a tapestry divine,
Vows exchanged beneath the love-light shine.
Her heart aflutter, emotions arrayed,
In silver and navy, love displayed.

But post the vows, a shift unseen,
The groom elusive, in shadows keen.
He vanished like mist in the warm sunlight,
A disappearance, a startling blight.

Outside he lingered, in solitude lost,

A silent tempest, a chilling frost.
Cake cutting delayed, a dance deferred,
His absence a whisper, love unheard.

The bride sought him in the moonlit glow,
In silvered whispers, her tears did flow.
He was out again, in shadows cast,
Love's dance disrupted, moments passed.

She found him, a phantom in the night,
An elusive groom, a love contrite.
A dance unshared, a cake untouched,
In the hushed aftermath, love clutched.

A disappearance, a heartache profound,
Love's celebration, in shadows drowned.
The bride, a captive of love's cruel jest,
In the echoes of absence, her heart distressed.

Farewell

At the threshold of intimacy, a moment's grace,
Anticipation hung, love in the space.
The bedroom awaited, a haven of trust,
But he tarried, a delay unjust.

I sought him out, in the dim-lit night,
A lover's embrace, a shared delight.
To the garage's shadows, my steps did wend,
A surreal journey, where illusions end.

In the corners of shadows, a scene revealed,
A shattered promise, love's fate sealed.
A needle's dance, a dance of despair,
A solemn vow shattered, suspended in air.

Waves of emotion, crashing, cascading,
In that moment, reality invading.
He had sworn, pledged a better way,
Yet in the garage's haze, promises lay.

Numbness embraced, a heart once warm,
Lost in shadows, in love's bitter storm.
The pain, a phantom, a haunting specter,
Love's demise, an unspoken vector.

No more tears to shed, a well run dry,

A final goodbye, a soul's goodbye.
Promises shattered, love's cruel jest,
In the garage's silence, a heart at rest.

Embrace the numbness, the cold refrain,
A heart untangled from love's cruel chain.
The bedroom's warmth turned cold and gray,
In that moment, I knew, I was finally away.

Part Two

A Tainted Start

In the realm of fresh beginnings, love unfurls,
Two hearts entwined, as if destined for the swirl.
She, with hopeful eyes, sees a chance anew,
A man promising the skies, vows sincere and true.

In the tapestry of their budding affair,
She paints the hues of love, free from despair.
He, a canvas of potential, a promise untold,
Yet beneath the surface, deception unfolds.

She, with scars from a love that once went awry,
Sought solace in his gaze, beneath the starry sky.
Actions spoke louder than words, or so she believed,
In the garden of trust, she planted seeds.

He, with whispers veiled in deceit,
Secret liaisons, a clandestine feat.
A betrayal concealed, a wound yet unseen,
In the heart of trust, a venomous sheen.

She uncovered the lie, the web he'd spun,
A clandestine dance that had just begun.
In the echoes of deceit, her heart recoiled,
A story of love, now tragically soiled.

"I can change," he pled with earnest eyes,

A masterful script, a manipulator's guise.
She, with a heart tender, longed to believe,
In the promise of change, she chose to cleave.

Yet, the path ahead, fraught with deceit,
His words, a mirage, a treacherous beat.
In the dance of manipulation, she twirled,
A captive soul in the chaos of a new world.

He spoke of transformation, a love reborn,
Yet, in the shadows, the same script worn.
A puppeteer's touch, a masterstroke,
In the fragile fabric of trust, he awoke.

She, ensnared in the siren's song,
A melody of change, deceptive and strong.
Yet, in the depths of her soul, a whisper persisted,
The truth obscured, the promise twisted.

In the dance of deceit, he held her tight,
A puppet and puppeteer, lost in the night.
Yet, as she wove dreams in the web of his lies,
A glimmer of truth flickered in her tearful eyes.

In the tapestry of love, she found a tear,
A rupture unseen, a wound laid bare.
For in the crucible of deceit and strife,
She yearned for a love, unburdened by disguise.

Near Death

In the tender cocoon of warmth, we lay,
A love once gentle, now spiraling astray.
Words whispered like promises, sweet and divine,
Yet beneath the surface, a tempest would twine.

A comment escaped, a temerarious phrase,
A trigger pulled, a storm ablaze.
In an instant, the sanctuary was stripped,
As his grip on my hair, like a serpent, gripped.

The pain, a lightning bolt, surged through my core,
As tears welled up, love's warmth was no more.
In the shadows, his anger brewed,
A symphony of cruelty, a love misconstrued.

He, a puppeteer, strings pulled with disdain,
A maestro of torment, orchestrating pain.
Names spat like venom, a toxic tirade,
As the sanctuary crumbled, love began to fade.

"Get out!" he roared, an echo of rage,
The love once tender, now trapped in a cage.
In the turmoil, I sought refuge in flight,
A silent plea, a desperate plight.

The room, a witness to love's decay,

As I gathered courage to walk away.
Yet, the air grew dense, a palpable threat,
As he brandished a gun, a dance with regret.

A barrel cold against my trembling head,
The metallic taste of fear, a prayer unsaid.
In the room, an eerie silence fell,
As the gun's shadow cast a nightmarish spell.

He, a puppeteer with power untold,
Manipulated my fear, a narrative bold.
I tried to escape, retrieve what was mine,
Yet the gun's cold touch told of love's malign.

In the dance of despair, my tears flowed,
A river of sorrow, a love erode.
The pain, a tapestry woven with dread,
As I walked on shards, my spirit bled.

"I'll pull the trigger," his words pierced the air,
A sinister threat, a heart's despair.
In the room, the shadows danced,
A macabre waltz, a love entranced.

In the clutches of fear, I moved like a ghost,
Retrieving my belongings, love's bitter boast.
He, a specter of anger, a phantom of hate,
The gun's cold gaze sealed love's cruel fate.

The room held echoes of love undone,
As I fled, my heart weighed by a loaded gun.
The scars, not just skin deep, a soul in decay,
In the aftermath of terror, I sought the light of day.

For in the crucible of pain, a phoenix must rise,
From the ashes of fear, reclaim the skies.

H. WALDON

In the tapestry of survival, a story to tell,
A journey from darkness to the light of farewell.

Blaze

A storm brewed in the twilight of deceit,
Lies unveiled, a truth bitter and discreet.
His anger, a tempest, a venomous surge,
As secrets emerged, the curtain did purge.

Caught in the crossfire of his wrath,
My heart trembled on a precarious path.
In the front yard, my clothes lay strewn,
Symbols of love, now a tale marooned.

The fabric of trust, ripped and torn,
In the wake of lies, love forlorn.
His rage, a wildfire, threatening to ignite,
As he cast my world into the unforgiving night.

Threads of deception, a tangled skein,
In the echoes of fury, love's refrain.
The threat lingered, an inferno's flare,
To set aflame the remnants of love's despair.

My heart, a hostage in the gathering storm,
Torn between fear and love's deform.
The clothes, like ghosts, whispered tales,
Of a love unraveling, as trust impales.

A pawn in the chessboard of his ire,

The threat of flames, a consuming pyre.
Emotions swirled, a chaotic ballet,
In the front yard, where love decayed.

 I stood, a witness to my world in flames,
The threat tangible, a perilous games.
In the unraveling fabric, I found my voice,
To break free from love's tormented choice.

 Yet the scars lingered, etched in fear,
As the flames of that night drew near.
In the debris of love, a phoenix yearned,
To rise from ashes, a lesson learned.

Signs

A walking tapestry of red flags, he appeared,
Yet blinded by love, the warnings she neared.
In the labyrinth of passion, she tread,
Overlooking signs that foretold the dread.

His words, a symphony of deceit and charm,
Yet in their melody, forebodings disarm.
Red flags fluttered in the gusts of despair,
Yet she sailed on, love's reckless affair.

The first flag unfurled, a warning flare,
In his temper's storm, love hung in the air.
She saw it, a tempest within his eyes,
Yet sailed past, beneath love's deceptive skies.

Flag by flag, they adorned his being,
Yet in love's haze, she kept from fleeing.
Manipulation danced in his every move,
A toxic waltz, a sinister groove.

A flag of possessiveness, crimson and bold,
Waved in the wind, a story untold.
Yet she, entrapped, in love's ensnaring thread,
Dismissed the warnings that reason shed.

His jealousy, a red flag's ominous hue,

Yet she painted it with love's transient glue.
In the shadows, doubts and fears grew,
As red flags whispered of love untrue.

Each warning ignored, each sign bypassed,
A love story written in flags, forecast.
She navigated through the stormy night,
Ignoring the flags, love's blinded flight.

In the echoes of heartache, hindsight's glow,
The red flags, a cruel afterglow.
Yet in the wreckage of love, lessons learned,
A phoenix rising, a soul discerned.

The Dent

Amidst the chaos of a drunken night,
His words a storm, a tempest's spite.
Yells and slurs, a torrential rain,
My heart weathered, a hurricane's strain.

I pulled the car to a trembling stop,
The moment hung, a precipice to drop.
"Get out," I commanded, a plea in my eyes,
Yet in his rage, reason defies.

He stumbled out, his fury untamed,
Kicking the car, a tempest untamed.
Metal groaned beneath his wrath,
A dent etched, a testament to the aftermath.

In the wake of his rage, the damage profound,
A car, a canvas, in chaos unbound.
I pleaded for respect, for repairs to make,
Yet his indifference, a silence did stake.

The reminder echoed, a refrain untold,
A damaged car, a story to unfold.
Yet respect, a currency he refused,
In the symphony of love, it remained unused.

A car, a symbol of the respect I sought,

In its dented side, love's battle fought.
He never fixed it, a testament clear,
To a love story marred by silent tears.

His lack of regard, a wound that bled,
In the tapestry of love, a thread left dead.
A dent, a scar on the car's alloy,
A metaphor for love's deep-seated ploy.

Respect, a plea lost in the night,
In the echoes of rage, love took flight.
I stood by the car, a silent plea,
For a love that respected, a soul set free.

The King

A king in his kingdom, or so he deemed,
A crown of greed, where his desires teemed.
A throne of entitlement, in shadows cast,
A realm of selfishness, love fading fast.

Always wanting, never willing to give,
A heart of avarice, a love narrative.
I, the servant, in his kingdom confined,
A giver of all, love's soul maligned.

He, the sovereign of endless demand,
A ruler of want, an insatiable hand.
No contributions offered, no sacrifices made,
In the kingdom of his greed, love began to fade.

I poured myself out, a vessel drained,
In the realm of his desires, I remained.
His appetite voracious, my offerings small,
A one-sided devotion, a love in thrall.

He expected worship, a regal decree,
A king in his castle, his desires set free.
Yet the more I gave, the more he took,
A love story unraveling, by greed mistook.

In the echoes of his demands, my voice grew weak,

A love story tainted, a soul left to speak.
The throne of greed, a lonely seat,
As I crumbled beneath love's cruel feat.

No reciprocity, no shared decree,
A kingdom of greed, where love ceased to be.
I, the servant, in shadows confined,
Yearning for a love, selflessly entwined.

A kingdom of one, his crown of disdain,
In the echoes of greed, love left in pain.
I, the giver, depleted and worn,
In the ruins of love, a heart forlorn.

Joy Becomes Despair

A fleeting escape, a girls' night in bloom,
A respite from shadows, a moment to consume.
Laughter echoed in the air, a reprieve from strife,
In the company of friends, I embraced life.

A year's weight lifted, a couple of hours mine,
Yet his texts punctured the joy, a subtle sign.
"Where are you?" he queried, impatience sown,
An ominous tone in each message known.

Catching up, savoring moments rare,
His impatience in texts, a rising flare.
"Almost done," I typed, my smile now strained,
A cloud of unease, my joy detained.

In the distance, his anger brewed,
The night still young, my joy subdued.
He left our house, a ghost in the night,
A shadow that fled, seeking respite.

To her house, the other woman, he steered,
A betrayal unveiled, a truth to be feared.
My heart, a casualty, in the games he played,
Sorrow eclipsed joy, in the choices he made.

The weight of abandonment, a soul laid bare,

In the aftermath of joy, a sudden despair.
He chose her over me, a truth exposed,
In the shadows of infidelity, love deposed.

His departure, a knife in the dark,
A pain that lingered, a relentless spark.
Alone in the night, betrayed and dismayed,
In the echoes of his absence, my happiness frayed.

A girls' night shattered, a moment's bliss,
Replaced by the ache of love's dark abyss.
In the void of his choice, sorrow entwined,
A heart broken, in the web of love maligned.

The Road You Take

Beneath the weight of shattered dreams,
I drowned in sorrow, lost at the seams.
A truth unveiled, a world unwound,
His lies and deceit, a love unsound.

In the bitter solace of a bottle's embrace,
I sought refuge, a fleeting grace.
Drinking deep, the pain to erase,
Yet reality lingered, a haunting trace.

On winding roads, my senses impaired,
A world of illusions, suddenly bared.
Around the curve, too swift to steer,
My car careened, fueled by despair.

In the middle of nowhere, darkness and cold,
The car halted, a story untold.
Driver's door sealed, a captive inside,
Crawling over the console, escaping the ride.

On foot, I stumbled, a journey distressed,
To our house down the road, a heart's request.
The night embraced me, shadows in flight,
Yet in my heart, an ominous night.

His absence echoed in the empty halls,

A house of secrets, crumbling walls.
I called his name, the phone in my hand,
A plea for solace, for someone to understand.

His voice, distant, a skeptical sneer,
He didn't believe, my words unclear.
In the tapestry of lies, a twisted design,
A truth rejected, love's painful malign.

The weight of betrayal, a heavy shroud,
In the silence that followed, love was avowed.
He, the architect of a world undone,
Left me stranded, in shadows to run.

The night stood witness to a heart's demise,
A drink-fueled escape, love's bitter prize.
His disbelief, a dagger in the dark,
A symphony of pain, an emotional mark.

In the aftermath, the wreckage revealed,
A woman broken, a love concealed.
The bottle's solace, a temporary balm,
Yet in the echoes, a love left disarmed.

Rose Colored Glasses

In shadows of deceit, she walks alone,
A heart entangled, a story overthrown.
His lies, a poison in love's delicate core,
Yet she clings, entwined, yearning for more.

He entered her world, a beacon of light,
After darkness subsided, after the night.
But light turned to shadows, love's cruel twist,
A tale of deception, a heart amiss.

Caught in a cycle, a web tightly spun,
Lies like silk, a battle never won.
Each revelation, a stab in the chest,
Yet she clings to hope, love's tragic quest.

In the echoes of betrayal, emotions collide,
A rollercoaster of love, a tempest inside.
He brought her joy, a fleeting delight,
Now he's the shadow that dims her light.

Why does she stay, in the face of despair?
A prisoner of fear, a love laid bare.
The hope he'll change, a fragile plea,
An anchor in chaos, love's desperate decree.

The light he brought, now a distant glow,

Yet she fears the dark, the unknown below.
Belief in a change, a mirage so clear,
In the labyrinth of fear, she's held near.

    A paradox of choices, a heart in strife,
Afraid to leave, to sever the life.
She convinces herself, there's nothing better out there,
A love-stricken captive, in the chains of despair.

    Scared to depart, from the familiar embrace,
To brave the unknown, to find her own space.
So she lingers, in the shadows of fear,
A captive soul, love's prisoner severe.

Exposed

In the glow of betrayal, a moment exposed,
I seized his phone, the secrets disclosed.
Messages clandestine, a web of deceit,
A narrative of infidelity, love's cruel feat.

He lunged for the device, a desperate plea,
But I fled outside, truth chasing me.
In the yard, shadows echoed my dread,
As he pursued me, a stormy thread.

A struggle ensued, a violent dance,
A push to the ground, a love's cruel trance.
Beneath his weight, the world blurred,
A symphony of pain, love unheard.

On the ground, pinned by his force,
He blamed me, the source of remorse.
For his dalliances, his deceitful charade,
A victim blamed, love's masquerade.

The phone, a weapon in his desperate clutch,
A struggle for truth, a desperate touch.
Held down, silenced by love's cruel game,
His anger a tempest, my soul aflame.

The blame, a poison, in his accusing eyes,

As he justified deceit, spun his web of lies.
On the ground, the world upside down,
A victim of love, a tarnished crown.

In that moment, love fractured and torn,
A dance of darkness, a soul reborn.
He took back the phone, but not the shame,
A heart scarred, love's enduring flame.

The pain lingered, etched in the night,
As he vanished, a specter in love's cruel light.
In the echoes of struggle, emotions concealed,
A woman broken, love's fate revealed.

Fractured

In the shadowed sanctuary of our bed,
A night unfolded, love hanging by a thread.
Words wielded like weapons, sharp and unkind,
His anger erupted, a tempest of the mind.

A comment innocuous, a spark to ignite,
His fury ablaze, a sudden bite.
Shoved off the bed, against the cold wall,
My head met its edge, a painful sprawl.

I rose with defiance, slapped in the air,
A rebellion against the growing despair.
His response swift, a punch to my jaw,
Love's descent, a broken law.

Pinned to the bed, his hands like a vice,
Around my throat, an act unwise.
Blame draped in fury, an ominous cloak,
He whispered, "Shut up," as my world broke.

In the echo of violence, love lay slain,
On the battleground of our shared domain.
Bruised and battered, a heart's silent cry,
In the hushed aftermath, a soul asked, "Why?"

The weight of sorrow, a crushing embrace,

In the twisted tangle of love and disgrace.
Silent screams, a night to forget,
As darkness settled, a soul beset.

He blamed my words, a dangerous art,
Yet in his violence, love fell apart.
The bed, a witness to a fractured trust,
A dance of pain, a soul unjust.

In the quiet of night, a sobbing refrain,
A woman broken, love's cruel terrain.
An oath to silence, a mouth tightly shut,
In the aftermath, a heart with a heavy gut.

Accused

A wandering soul in the shadows I tread,
Lost in a maze where my heart has bled.
His words like daggers, a relentless refrain,
I am the problem, the root of love's disdain.

A toxic tango, a dance of despair,
He points his fingers, blames my share.
In the mirror, I see the wreckage unfold,
Believing his words, a story retold.

Lost in the labyrinth of self-blame,
My heart shattered, consumed by shame.
His accusations, a cruel art,
Tearing apart the fabric of my heart.

I believed him, the puppeteer's skill,
In the theater of blame, I played my ill.
A broken record, a haunting song,
Believing I'm the problem, in love gone wrong.

Each accusation, a wound deep and raw,
I internalize the blame, an emotional flaw.
A puppet to his words, I dance in pain,
Convinced I'm the reason for love's disdain.

In the silent echoes of a breaking heart,

I play my part in this toxic art.
Lost in the narrative he weaves,
A soul adrift, believing in deceives.

The toxicity seeps, a venomous stream,
His words a nightmare, a recurring dream.
I feel so lost, a ghost in despair,
Haunted by blame, drowning in the air.

Yet, in the depths, a spark remains,
A yearning for freedom from love's cruel chains.
I must find strength, a path to mend,
For the lost heart to find love again.

Hidden Truth

Beneath the surface, a love unbound,
A tale of shadows where pain is found.
His charm, a mask to the world's eye,
Yet behind closed doors, a tempest's cry.

My father's gaze, affectionate and warm,
Unaware of the tempest, the emotional storm.
His love extends to the one who harms,
In the secret realm of twisted charms.

Bruises concealed, a secret so deep,
Beneath the smiles, where secrets creep.
A busted lip, a painful refrain,
Yet I guard the truth, love's bitter chain.

In silence I suffer, a heavy heart,
A canvas of bruises, a silent art.
The secrets held, a burden to bear,
Aching to reveal, yet caught in despair.

Wanting to tell, to break the walls,
But fear of judgment, pity that appalls.
I crave understanding, not sympathy's gaze,
To escape the shadows, love's binding maze.

The weight of silence, a heavy shroud,

A web of secrets, screaming loud.
Yearning for freedom, yet ensnared,
In the complexities of love, emotions bared.

　　It's not just the bruises, the physical scars,
But the wounds within, like emotional bars.
To speak my truth, to unshackle the chain,
Yet fear holds me back, in love's dark terrain.

　　The dance of secrecy, the twisted embrace,
A yearning for freedom, a silent grace.
In shadows I linger, in silence I weep,
A soul entangled, in love's secrets deep.

Part Three

The Master

In the kingdom of control, a man ensnared,
His dominion ruled by an iron-willed affair.
A puppeteer of emotions, a puppet in strings,
His grip, a vice, where autonomy stings.

Every word, a decree, a calculated command,
A symphony of control, conducted by his hand.
In the shadows of dominance, hearts entwined,
A narrative of control, a story unkind.

He wields influence with a tyrant's might,
A dictator in love, shadows in the light.
In the dance of emotions, his steps aligned,
A puppet master, love's autonomy maligned.

His gaze, a sentinel, scrutinizing the free,
In the labyrinth of control, no sanctuary to flee.
Each breath measured, each action observed,
Love's liberty, a notion undeserved.

She, a captive in his kingdom of command,
Invisible chains, emotions at his demand.
The walls closing in, a fortress of control,
In the kingdom's depths, a tormented soul.

His whispers of authority echo loud,

A love story tainted, a heart unbowed.
She yearns for autonomy, a liberated plea,
But in the kingdom of control, she's not free.

His love, a suffocation, a breath constrained,
In the fortress of control, emotions detained.
A symphony of intensity, a heart's dire toll,
In the man's realm, where control takes its hold.

Untamed

Resilience, a fire within, born from life's cruel design,
A mosaic of scars, each story a line.
He seeks to mold, to shape, to dictate,
But within my core, a spirit won't abate.

From the ashes of battles, a phoenix takes flight,
Each trial a testament, a war-worn sight.
In the echoes of trauma, a fortress I've built,
Against his control, my spirit is quilt.

He hungers for dominion, a puppet in hand,
But the threads of control can't tie what's been spanned.
In the crucible of life, I've learned to resist,
His attempts to subdue, I staunchly persist.

The grip he desires slips through his fingers,
A strength, a defiance, that eternally lingers.
His infuriation grows with each breath I take,
For a free spirit, his dominance can't break.

I am not a canvas for his desires to paint,
Not a vessel for his will to taint.
He craves submission, compliance, a bow,
Yet I stand tall, unbowed, I avow.

Past wounds have sculpted this fortress of mine,

Each scar, a testament to the strength I define.
He thinks he can master, impose his decree,
But my spirit resists, yearning to be free.

His frustration simmers, a tempest within,
As my strength weathers the storm, an enduring din.
He can't fathom the essence that fuels my might,
In the face of control, I stand in the light.

His attempts to shackle, to silence my voice,
Only amplify the strength of my choice.
I won't succumb to the chains he would weave,
For a spirit unbroken, he can't deceive.

In the tapestry of control, my defiance is sown,
A legacy of strength, in independence grown.
He may rage against the currents that surge,
But my spirit prevails, an unyielding urge.

He may seethe in frustration, his power denied,
Yet in my independence, my strength resides.
For I am not a captive, a pawn in his game,
I am the flame that refuses to tame.

He may crave control, a conquest to gain,
Yet against my spirit, his efforts are in vain.
In the dance of dominance, my steps are my own,
For a spirit untamed, cannot be overthrown.

Empty

A promisesmith he claims to be, yet his pledges are frail,
Words adorned in deception, an unreliable trail.
He dances on the precipice of commitment,
But his steps are fleeting, a transient sentiment.

The canvas of assurance, painted with deceit,
A masterpiece of untruths, where sincerity's defeat.
He speaks of tomorrows, a kaleidoscope of dreams,
Yet the morrow's sun reveals unfulfilled schemes.

In the tapestry of trust, his threads are thin,
A fabric woven with whims, a promise left to spin.
Each word, a feather in the wind's swift grasp,
Lost in the currents, trust's fragile clasp.

He builds a bridge of assurances, a structure so frail,
A span of unfulfilled vows, a bridge set to fail.
His promises, like autumn leaves, flutter and fall,
A cascade of disappointments, a trust's burial.

The clock ticks to the rhythm of his hollow words,
A melody of letdowns, a chorus unheard.
He claims allegiance to duty and devotion,
Yet his actions echo a different emotion.

Untrustworthy whispers in the corridors of time,

His words echo, but their resonance is a mime.
The trust he erodes, a subtle erosion,
A silent dismantling, a commitment's corrosion.

His intentions may sparkle, a deceptive sheen,
But the substance is lacking, a mirage unseen.
The bridge he promised, a path to reliance,
Yet each plank crumbles, a pledge in defiance.

In the garden of trust, his seeds lay barren,
A harvest of falsehoods, a trust unchosen.
He may speak of commitment with a practiced flair,
Yet the seeds he sows are but promises in thin air.

A storyteller of pledges, a narrator untamed,
Yet his tales lack substance, his integrity maimed.
The landscape of trust bears scars of his touch,
A tapestry unraveling, a vow's bitter clutch.

In the saga of reliability, his chapter is writ,
A script of broken promises, a tale unfit.
He may wear the cloak of commitment with grace,
Yet actions reveal truth, a trust's final embrace.

Anguish

Regret, a bitter pill in the hollows of my soul,
In the tapestry of choices, a narrative takes its toll.
I crafted a haven, a sanctuary of dreams,
But in the silence, a symphony of unheard screams.

He plays his games, an escape from reality,
While I dance attendance, a silent formality.
Bearing burdens of bills, piled high as the sky,
Yet his gratitude remains a perpetual goodbye.

A mother, a student, a juggler of life,
Yet in his eyes, my efforts are but a strife.
I've bought him treasures, things we can't afford,
Yet his ungrateful heart cuts, a double-edged sword.

Video games claim his post-work affection,
While I cradle responsibilities, a lone reflection.
A child to tend, with each coo and cry,
Yet my studies dismissed, a plaintive sigh.

He deems my pursuits, my dreams, a waste,
Yet in the classroom, my aspirations are encased.
He believes my attention falters, a misguided view,
But in the library's hush, my focus rings true.

I watch the baby, amidst textbooks and notes,

Yet his dissatisfaction in every silence floats.
Schoolwork neglected, as his games take flight,
In the shadows of resentment, I strive to write.

Video after video, a screen's cold glow,
His escape pursued, in the dark's ebb and flow.
What does he contribute to this life we've made?
An ungrateful partner, a decision delayed.

Bills pile higher, a crescendo of despair,
Yet his obsessions persist, a relentless affair.
He lays in bed, a passive spectator,
While responsibilities mount, an unequal specter.

I've stretched the budget, contorted and bent,
In the labyrinth of debt, my regrets are sent.
He cradles controllers, in virtual bliss,
While reality's burdens I cannot dismiss.

An education sought, a path to empower,
Yet his disdain grows with each passing hour.
He echoes that I'm failing, falling behind,
Yet his failures, a silence unkind.

Regret, a shadow in the dim-lit room,
A specter of choices, shrouded in gloom.
I ponder the paths, the decisions untold,
In the tapestry of regret, my story unfolds.

In the quiet corners, where sorrow resides,
I question the choices, where happiness hides.
Ungrateful echoes linger, a haunting refrain,
As I navigate the labyrinth, a soul in pain.

Greed

Selfish echoes in the chambers of my heart,
A poignant melody tearing dreams apart.
His desires, a voracious flame,
Devouring the love that once held its claim.

In the realm of us, he stands alone,
A king of his own, on a heartless throne.
His needs precede, a relentless decree,
While mine crumble, a silent plea.

A symphony of wants, his insatiable song,
Yet my needs, drowned, silent and long.
He consumes attention, an endless feast,
While my hunger for love remains unceased.

His world revolves around his own,
In the center, a selfish heart, a heart of stone.
The tapestry of us, once vibrant and bright,
Now dulls under the weight of his selfish might.

I paint our story with strokes of compromise,
But in his canvas, only his desires arise.
He gazes at the reflection of his needs,
While my reflection in his eyes recedes.

His time, a currency spent on selfish whims,

Leaving me with remnants of stolen glims.
The laughter we shared, now a distant recall,
In the shadow of selfishness, love's downfall.

I offered my heart, a gift untold,
Yet in his hands, my love's value he sold.
A transaction of emotions, love's currency spent,
A selfish act, a selfless sentiment.

He harvests pleasure from love's barren field,
Leaving me with wounds that refuse to heal.
In the garden of us, his selfish seeds sown,
Leaving me to tend love's garden alone.

His needs, like shadows, eclipse my light,
A perpetual dusk in love's fading night.
He drinks from the cup of self-serving desire,
While my cup overflows with love's quenched fire.

I linger in the corridors of love's decay,
As his selfish choices lead love astray.
Yet, in the ruins of what used to be,
A whisper of hope, a plea to be free.

I see the reflection of a once hopeful face,
Now etched with the lines of love's own disgrace.
His selfishness, a dagger in love's side,
Leaving me with wounds too deep to hide.

Yet, in the echoes of heartbreak's sad refrain,
A resilience emerges, a strength to sustain.
For love may crumble, but it also rebuilds,
In the ruins of selfishness, hope distills.

I stand in the aftermath of love's cruel strife,
Learning to navigate the contours of a transformed life.

His selfish choices may have left me torn,
But in the mending, a woman reborn.

The Illusion

Exploited echoes in the chambers of my heart,
A symphony of pain tearing my world apart.
In the guise of love, a deception profound,
Yet all that remains is an empty, echoing sound.

His touch, a transaction, not love's gentle embrace,
A fleeting connection, a cold, distant space.
My heart, an offering on love's sacrificial pyre,
Yet in his eyes, it's just fuel for his desire.

I feel used, like a pawn in a heartless game,
His affection a facade, a fleeting flame.
His love, a currency, spent on selfish need,
Leaving me with wounds that silently bleed.

My heartbreak is an anthem, a sorrowful song,
In the verses of deceit, where trust went wrong.
His love, a mirage, a desert mirroring heat,
Leaving me parched, love's defeat.

I offered him my soul, a gift untold,
Yet in his hands, its value he'd withhold.
His affection, a transactional decree,
Leaving me questioning what love should be.

I'm a vessel for his wants, desires, and whims,

Yet when my heart calls, he's deaf to its hymns.
Used and discarded, a soul worn and torn,
In the crucible of his love, I'm left forlorn.

His love, a conditional plea,
Dependent on what he can take from me.
A heart once full, now echoes in despair,
A silent scream in love's vacant air.

It breaks me, the realization profound,
That his love is a facade, a hallow sound.
I'm a pawn in his game, a means to an end,
A heart's betrayal, a trusted friend.

In the ruins of this love, I stand alone,
Used, discarded, my heart overthrown.
Yet from the ashes, strength will rise,
A phoenix of resilience, despite love's lies.

The Puppeteer

Manipulated, I dance in shadows of deceit,
His fingers, puppet strings, make my heart beat.
A maestro of lies, he orchestrates the game,
I, the captive note, in his melody of shame.

Gaslight whispers weave a web so fine,
Invisible threads, his intricate design.
He paints my actions in hues of wrong,
A canvas of confusion, where I don't belong.

His words, like knives, cut through my truth,
Twisting reality, distorting my youth.
I walk on eggshells, afraid to step wrong,
In the labyrinth of manipulation, I'm lost, not strong.

Every smile, a mask, concealing his control,
A marionette dance, he plays the role.
I question my sanity in this mind-bending show,
As he convinces me I'm the cause of this woe.

He twists my words, a sinister game,
A master manipulator, with no sense of shame.
I second-guess every thought, every action,
Caught in the web of his calculated reaction.

Crazy, he whispers, like a venomous spell,

A label that echoes, a self-made hell.
Gasping for air in this toxic atmosphere,
I drown in the doubts he plants, crystal clear.

A puppeteer of emotions, he pulls the strings tight,
Controlling the narrative, dimming my light.
I become a reflection of his distorted view,
A distorted mirror, fractured and askew.

Every apology I utter, a surrender to his game,
Yet, his demands for control remain the same.
I navigate a maze of psychological dismay,
In this manipulated reality, I lose my way.

He frames my faults in the gallery of his mind,
Each brushstroke a condemnation, unkind.
Gaslight shadows dance, a twisted ballet,
As I struggle to find the words to convey.

A victim in this play, a pawn on his board,
In the symphony of manipulation, I'm the discord.
Yet, in the shadows, a flicker of strength emerges,
A silent rebellion, as the manipulated soul converges.

I untangle the threads, though they cut like knives,
Reclaiming my narrative, reclaiming my lives.
No longer the puppet in his calculated strife,
I step into the light, reclaiming my life.

The Final Echo

Estranged echoes in the corridors of their shared life,
A marriage unraveling, stitched wounds from endless strife.
He wielded the threat of divorce, a weapon so unkind,
She, a captive audience, weary in heart and mind.

In the tumult of their battles, he brandished the word,
Divorce, a dagger, its edge serrated and absurd.
Promises shattered, like glass upon cold stone,
A sanctuary once cherished, now love overthrown.

She, worn by the constant threat's relentless sting,
A captive to his whims, the pendulum on a string.
His words, a torrent of pain, a relentless cascade,
Yet in her heart, a quiet rebellion was made.

Tired of the constant shadow, the impending fall,
She grasped at the remnants of her own emotional wall.
Decisions weighed heavy, yet a fire sparked within,
No longer would she be confined, a soul worn thin.

She faced the mirror, reflecting on her worth,
A decision crystallized, the most profound rebirth.
The papers filed, a testament to her release,
Yet in the aftermath, the storm only found its increase.

Once the news reached his ears, a tempest unfurled,

He recoiled in shock, as the ground beneath him swirled.
The tables turned, yet he played the victim's role,
Blaming her for the decision that took a heavy toll.

It wasn't his constant threats that pushed her to the brink,
But the toxicity of their union, an abyss in which they sink.
He feigned innocence, denied the blame he bore,
As if divorce was a surprise, not part of the metaphor.

The courtroom became a stage, their grievances laid bare,
Yet his protests, a performance, devoid of true despair.
She stood resolute, reclaiming fragments of her soul,
The divorce decree signed, an ending to the toll.

In the aftermath, emotions lingered, an echo's trace,
A blend of relief and sorrow etched on her face.
No longer captive to threats, a newfound liberty,
She walked away from the storm, toward her own decree.

Duality

Unpredictable shadows cloak our shared domain,
A rollercoaster ride through joy and searing pain.
He, a complex concoction of Jekyll and Hyde,
A kaleidoscope of emotions, a turbulent tide.

Nervous whispers echo through the hollows of my heart,
His moods, a tempest, tearing my world apart.
Dr. Jekyll's warmth, a fleeting embrace,
Yet Mr. Hyde's cruelty leaves no trace.

Anxiety thrives in the spaces between,
The unpredictability, a relentless unseen.
A moment of kindness, a transient high,
Followed by heartlessness, a soul's bitter sigh.

His accusations, a mirror turned askew,
Reflecting his actions, not the truth he knew.
He accuses me of hearts unfeeling,
Yet his emotional pendulum keeps on swinging.

Stress becomes a silent companion in our abode,
The tension thickens, like an unspoken code.
His laughter, a respite, soon turns to disdain,
In the cyclone of emotions, I'm left in the rain.

I navigate the minefield of his shifting mood,

An emotional tightrope, where my steps are pursued.
One minute, a lover with eyes so kind,
The next, a stranger, with a heart unaligned.

I'm the accused in this courtroom of strife,
Yet his shifting demeanor holds the sharpest knife.
Heartless, he labels me, a cruel decree,
As I dance to the erratic beats of his emotional sea.

I yearn for stability, a sanctuary of calm,
Yet his emotional tempest is a relentless psalm.
The label of heartlessness, a twisted reflection,
In this volatile love, an endless dissection.

The waves of uncertainty crash against my shore,
His emotional volatility, a tempest's roar.
Stress etches lines on my once-smooth skin,
In this chaotic love, where to end, where to begin?

I question my sanity in this topsy-turvy ride,
His mood swings, a carnival, where emotions hide.
Yet, in the midst of chaos, a resolve takes seed,
To break free from the cycles, a desperate need.

His heart's duality, a puzzle unsolved,
In the labyrinth of love, our story evolved.
I, a captive to the whims of his erratic side,
Yet within the chaos, a strength will abide.

As I navigate the turbulence of love's bitter brew,
I yearn for stability, a love that rings true.
In the echoes of unpredictability, I find my way,
To break free from this heart's disarray.

Writing these poems were not easy, and neither was publishing for the world to see. I hope my story helps others see that you are truly not alone.

This is the first publication of H. Waldon.

www.ingramcontent.com/pod-product-compliance
Lightning Source LLC
Chambersburg PA
CBHW071644170726
48000CB00024B/2130